MUSIC
APPRECIATION

To Scott,
with regards +
Thanks for the visit

Floyd Skloot
Amity OR
10/2000

University of Central Florida • *Contemporary Poetry Series*

MUSIC
APPRECIATION

Floyd Skloot

University Press of Florida

Gainesville / Tallahassee / Tampa / Boca Raton
Pensacola / Orlando / Miami / Jacksonville

99 98 97 96 95 94   6 5 4 3 2 1

Library of Congress Cataloging-in-Publication Data

Skloot, Floyd.
Music appreciation / Floyd Skloot.
p.   cm. — (University of Central Florida contemporary
poetry series)
ISBN 0–8130–1313–5 (cloth). — ISBN 0–8130–1314–3 (pbk.)
I. Title.   II. Series: Contemporary poetry series (Orlando, Fla.)
PS3569.K577M87   1994   94–26085
811'.54—dc20

The University Press of Florida is the scholarly publishing agency for the State
University System of Florida, comprised of Florida A & M University, Florida
Atlantic University, Florida International University, Florida State University,
University of Central Florida, University of Florida, University of North Florida,
University of South Florida, and University of West Florida.

University Press of Florida
15 Northwest 15th Street
Gainesville, FL 32611

For my children
Matthew and Rebecca

CONTENTS

ACKNOWLEDGMENTS

Grateful acknowledgment is made to the editors of the following magazines, in which some of these poems first appeared:

Aisling, American Scholar, Calapooya Collage, Chelsea, Chronicles, Cincinnati Poetry Review, Commonweal, Confrontation, Crazyhorse, Gettysburg Review, Hubbub, Madison Review, Mississippi Mud, New Criterion, New England Review & Bread Loaf Quarterly, North Dakota Quarterly, Northwest Review, Paintbrush, Poet & Critic, Poetry, Poetry East, Poetry Northwest, Prairie Schooner, Seattle Review, Shenandoah, Southern Poetry Review, Southwest Review, Tendril.

"You Asked for It" was reprinted in *Harper's,* January 1988. "Brain Scan," "Diagnostic Imaging," "Home Remedies," "Music Appreciation," "A Softer Place," "The View" and "The Virus" were reprinted in *JAMA: The Journal of the American Medical Association.*

Some of these poems appeared in the chapbooks *Rough Edges* (Chowder Chapbooks, 1979), *Kaleidoscope* (Silverfish Review Press, 1986), and *Wild Light* (Silverfish Review Press, 1989). My thanks to their editors, Ron Slate and Rodger Moody.

I would also like to acknowledge the Illinois Arts Council and the Oregon Institute of Literary Arts for fellowships, and Centrum for a residency, during the time many of these poems were written.

I
THE FURY

LIVING ROOM

I thought the face of Beethoven glaring
between our piano and easy chair
was my father when he was young. Staring
till his eyes dried up, sparking the wild hair
that would soon fly completely off his head,
my father even then was a wizard
of silent menace, a genius of dread.
He saw me. He knew what I did. He heard
the music of my musings. My mother
played Gershwin oblivious of the scorn
singing along would bring down on me. Her
smile froze, her eyes slowly closed, her voice worn
down by years of smoke broke into sobs when
she lost herself in the old melody.
Not me. I sat beside her silently.

CHICKEN MARKET

He parted the doors at four.
By eight the sawdusted floors
were patched with clots of feathers

and blood. I felt their lumps
under my soles all day.
The faces of three scales

flung sunlight out
and bulbs hung every ten
feet became stars

when I squinted. Ladies
would nod at the aproned man,
my father, with flannel bunched

at his biceps. When an order
was placed, his hand would burst
into the coop, making cries

ricochet. It snatched a capon's
feet and swept him face
down through the gate.

Wrists snapping, arms
flapping faster than wings,
he wrapped the legs above

the spurs with wire and dangled
the capon from the scale's hook
shouting "four pounds

six" over his shoulder.
Nod. Back by the cans
to the plucker, who thrust it,

squawking blood, legs
kicking air, slit
neck in first to die.

The capon came back,
a spotted brown package,
taped shut, and the sale was rung.

RHAPSODY IN CALICO (1925)

On a morning
so bright it made roses
bloom in her upswept hair

near noontime
in America's first summer
of crossword puzzles
and The Charleston

my mother in a two
piece calico sunsuit
posed on one foot

a mottled heron
amid the lush foliage
of Central Park

her left hand
spread to hide her navel

her mouth shut
to hide her teeth

only her eyes
open to the camera

knowing there should be
wind moving the leaves
at her bare shoulder

current in the still water
whose surface gives back
too much light

moss on the rock beside her

at the very least
a blur of blackbirds
aflutter on the edges
of this picture

some sign of life
other than the one leaf
reaching from the bank

pretending to lose
itself like a man
in the pattern she wore

THE SUNDAY CHEF

With one hand my father cracked
eggshells on the jam jar's lip
and with a quick dip let
the yolks slip through whole.
Next he shook two drops of hot
pepper sauce into the heart
of each yolk and pierced it
with a fork. The yellow ooze
had nowhere to flow. It rose
as though breathing and pooled.

When he poured on a fist of salt
I saw the same smile he wore
at work—saw the knife he held
in one fist gleam, saw the chicken's
neck clenched in the other, then
his brisk slitting of its throat.

Before I knew it his swift look
above the lifted drink caught me,
saw me shudder at the raw egg
in a flashing of his glass eye.
The smile faded as he reached
across the space between us
and pressed the rim to my lips.

THE PRICE IS RIGHT

One March morning in 1958
my mother guessed the price of a brand new
split-level on Long Island. It is fate,
she thought, God knows we need it. She could do
nothing wrong that half-hour. She got the trip
to Florence, doublewall Amana range,
classic fox stole. Hardly daring to sip
her Savarin, she sat still in the strange
chill of pure luck, conceiving another
life. She whispered the precise figure for
a baby grand; there would be song. Mother
would host luncheons on the patio or
soirees in the sand. Then the show ended.
Her fortunes left her as they always did.

BEAT THE CLOCK

I remember my father's hand
going up. Then blonde Roxanne came
to kneel beside him for our name.
Mother reminded me to stand
still when Bud Collyer spoke and smile.
They all said I would have to run
fast and not look at the clock. One
minute is no time at all.
                              While
my father was setting off small
mousetraps with a hot dog tied to
a fishing pole, I had to undo
the sprung traps, trying not to fall
as I raced to the next, halfway
across stage. We did six and earned
the right to go again.
                        I turned
to look offstage when asked to say
what kind of pie I liked because
we didn't eat desserts at home.
Roxanne brought a tin heaped with cream.
I licked the top before I tossed
it at the cigar someone stuck
between my father's teeth. It fell
short. The next splattered his lapel.
The third was far enough but struck
his cheek. With ten seconds to go,
I hit the cigar flush and we
advanced to the bonus stunt.

He
and I were the stars of the show.
People cheered, the band held its note,
and I blew up balloons he tied
as the big clock ticked down and I
stuffed them inside his baggy coat.

MORNING SHADOWS

—Brooklyn, NY

My brother slept with one eye
    open wide,
the eye's center all pupil,
    the pupil
itself open in all light,
his sight filling with darkness.

My brother turned in his sleep
    like the tide,
woke with his back to the wall,
    the long beach
of his bed darkened with dried
sweat, the air thick with his dreams,
sharp as the long shard of glass
    that took his
sight from the eye that never
    could stay closed.

We shared a room with morning
    shadows, light
that seeped between wings of brick
    to find us
no matter where we had been,
no matter where we thought we
    were going.

My brother never told me
    that he dreamed

what I had dreamed, that he knew
          between us
and our sleeping parents was
          the last safe
place we would know, a narrow
space lit by the thinnest hope.

My brother moved through his days
          without me,
moved into a life so far
from our room we had nothing
          left but this
long silence that divides us.

SMOKE

My father's long cigar suffused the car
with smoke that slowly absorbed my mother's
paler Chesterfield smoke. They formed a far
harsher smoke together than each other's
on its own. The Buick's windows stayed closed
against a tousling winter wind and I
could only breathe small, the way I supposed
a fish on land must, trying not to die.

Of course, I knew their smoke would never kill
me. Smoke made lungs strong, which made voices strong
and charged the whole body till it was filled
with force. Parents needed force for the long
drives where they fought those battles that did not
get fought at home. I was there to breathe smoke
for the future, learn to skirmish, see what
love was. I never coughed. I never spoke.

RUBY FOO'S

Looking at me
in her bedroom mirror,
squinting through smoke
as she tied a violet scarf,
Mother said I could wear
the new boatneck shirt
she bought for summer camp.
I should let its tail
hang over my belt.

Alone in my room
I became exotic—
the shirt, pure
chic, would make me fit
company for Mother in
her flowing cape.
Rapture of Thursday
night theater might
someday be mine.

But in the foyer
Father kicked me in
the ass for failing
to tuck the shirttail in.
Hiss of their whispered
fighting quieted me
where I hid in
a curl of drape.

Apology was a change
of plans, dinner

at Ruby Foo's instead
of grandmother's living
room. I could eat lobster
Cantonese instead of flanken
with red horseradish.

Father's fork scratching
the silvery platter
slick with remains
of subgum pork chow mein
helped him explain how
ice water acts when bellies
are filled with Chinese food.

The sound
made me shiver,
but Father thought
seeing the oil globbed
in water finally taught
me to drink hot tea.
He cracked fortune
cookies for me to read
and leaned back,
snapping his fingers
for a check.

He and Mother
walked arm in arm to
the door while I
lingered at our table
trying to quench
a nightlong thirst
when no one was looking.

DINNERTIME

My mother's voice was drumfire
peppering my father home.
With his visor down,
my father's voice seeped
from his helmet like gas.

The choked hall
from their room to mine
was a trench packed firm
by crawling for cover.
String I could not reach
was a wisp of hope dangling
from the attic door.

Their silence was the signal
that dinnertime had come,
a shaky cease-fire
meaning eat while you can.

TWILIGHT TIME

—The Platters
Spring, 1958

It could only be
a dream since the drapes
are tied back, there is lilac
sunset above rooftops and Sabbath
candles flicker in their saucers
just for play. How else
could there be rhythm
and blues on the Victrola
at dusk? My mother softly
sets the needle arm down
and turns to smile at him
through the static, spreading
her feathered boa like angels'
wings before gliding
into my father's arms.

His easy chair has floated
away, the sea of carpet
has parted and oak dark
as the earth's heart holds
them. I know it is only
in dreams that their hands
touch and twine, that shades
of night would bring them
together like this.
All that is impossible
is that it could have happened.

They move to the smooth blend
of the singers' voices, love
is in their eyes, their separate
days are given up to a mellow
music. Now they are twirling,
together at last at twilight time.

THE EVERLY BROTHERS

My brother thought they were freaks
of nature, voices fitting together
through some fluke of chemistry.
He said they might just as well
have been Siamese twins sharing
a heart, or the Everly humpbacks.

My brother preferred Jerry
Lee Lewis and Chuck Berry.
He cackled at their antics,
battering mother's baby
grand with his fists when we
were alone and duckwalking
the hallway until our downstairs
neighbors hit their ceiling
with a broom. At night he worked
on his Elvis sneer while caking
his face with Clearasil.

I can still see my brother
rave as we rode four stories
up in the quaking elevator.
He offered me one frenzied
groove of Yakety Yak at the top
of his lungs when I tried
to sing. All I wanted was
his voice joining mine in
harmony. The song did not
have to be about faith in love.

THE CLUES

Because it is Brooklyn
Father is still alive.

I think it is a morning
in 1952. I can look from bed
to the facing wing, down
a brick alcove four stories
high. Because his room has two
windows, he and Mother sleep
separately. Because she remains
asleep, I straddle his huge
middle to hammer at his belly.
He strains to keep
from laughing loud enough
to wake her. Because he brings
a man home to play balalaika,
he is ready to sell his market.

Because we can hear waves
break on the beach a block
away, he limps and has thinned.
Because there are steps
it takes time to climb
he turns to watch me
pitch to a friend.

It is daytime yet
he is home. He hefts
his cane like a bat.

STILL LIFE WITHOUT FATHER

The reading lamp beside his easy chair
is lit, its tassels wreathed by cigar smoke
rising from an abalone shell. Poised there
like whitecaps, waves of paper wrappers poke
from their empty box of butterscotch cremes.
The latest *Life* is spread like a doily
across the soiled chairback where his head seems
to have been.
             Shut drapes suggest it may
be winter, although there is no steaming glass
of Lipton's tea, no black cardigan, no
plaid-covered flask of brandy.
                    Time will pass
without changing the life these objects show,
caught between a time his memory sits
within and a shape his lost image fits.

WIDOW'S MORNING

This day of all days
she must not sleep
past early afternoon—

She dreamed a crackling bolt
that cleaved their bed
burst his half into flames.
Hers became clear lakewater
beneath a sapphirine sky,
turning slowly
as the charged air
sparked with strokes of light.

She wakes face up
as she would never sleep
in a room turning luminous
wondering what people do
with their mornings—

The Jamaican maid
will not let herself in
at nine nor time
peppermint tea for the soaps today.

On her own
she finds the spot
sunlight warms first
is the seat her husband's form
wore smooth through decades
of whole wheat toast

and marmalade at dawn.
Eggs he'd never eat
she coddles now
the way her mother taught her,
gazing in the oven glass
while they bubble and settle.

Sausage once a week,
roast pullet with new
potatoes and pearl onions
every Friday since '39,
apple the only fruit.

Now November spreads
before her like a smorgasbord—
but its odors suggest
organ meat boiled for stock
and cheap cuts
disguised with marinara.
She leans
over the sink
steamy with dishwater,
her stillness
frightening the son
in his dark gabardine
till he sees
she is gauging the tints
of her crisply frosted hair
in the toaster's chrome.

She stubs out her cigarette
when the car doors
of the first mourners slam.
Feather duster in hand,

trailing scents
of tobacco and pine oil,
she stomps down the two steps
to their marble hearth
where no fire burned
all the years they lived there.
She folds a towel
against the cold
and kneels.

SWIMMER

My mother swam with her feet
  on the pool floor.
Her one-piece brown suit billowed
  like a lily
pad when she bobbed with her breath
  scarcely rippling
the surface. Her hands circling
  as if over
Sabbath candles, her eyes shut,
  she went nowhere.

  I can still see
her in the shallow water,
  smooth black cap in
contrast to her usual
  pouf of tinted
hair, soft neck flesh glistening.
  Lips no longer
  done crimson, rapt
in a mermaid fantasy,
Mother would dream of suitors.

  After Father
died, she sought a valorous
  captain or full
professor, ruler of tracts
  in southern Greece,
Israeli surgeon fluent
  in Portuguese.
No more butchers in her life.

She gave herself five seasons
    to cruise and tour.

I would always wish her home
    as I had wished
her gone, ready in my fierce
    adolescence
to be troubled Prince to her
    Queen. She returned
Downcast, the world no solace
    for a sudden
widow with a teenage son.

THE ALBUM

This was the young man she should have married,
taller than my father and a full head
of hair. I can see how well he carried
himself, can't I? Poised and at ease instead
of coiled for flight. She knows who I get that
from! Or this: a friend of Jackson Pollock,
who could appreciate her as they sat
through long summery evenings of Dvořák.
They rowed on Schroon Lake and sipped lemon tea.

Or this son of money, so loyal to
his aging mother. He would go to see
her, never dream of living as I do
a continent away from the woman
who bore him. Even today she can see
how he greeted his mother, arms laden
with small gifts, happy as a man could be.

All those wonderful boys to choose among
and she chose my father with his flat nose,
his bent ears and one glass eye. Neither young
nor versed in the fine arts. Do I suppose
it was just passion? Any one of those
men! Then she smiles and says, simply, God knows.

THE FURY

Father drove his huge
black Buicks through
city streets at speeds
that tripped the heart.
Mother sat beside him
asserting where to turn.

Every two years
a new Buick—
their bodies never given
the chance to fail him.

After Father's heart
failed, Mother learned
to drive. She mastered
start and stop but not
turn. Her one car was
white. I sat beside her
waiting to come of age.

In those oceanfront years
the body of Mother's old
Fury wore away, shore air
cankering its skin like anger.
When she slammed the car
into park it rocked in place,
steam fuming from its hood.
That was what I learned
to drive, Mother beside me
shuddering at every turn.

It brought back
our city years with Father
alive. Sabbath suppers
erupted in shrieks, Mother
fleeing to sob behind her
slammed bedroom door.
I saw the thin candles
flicker in her rage,
the pullet sag
on its pallet of braised
fennel, and Father bow
his head to its vapors.

It brought back
the years of fear,
when we washed and washed
hands, never kissed lips,
the years of mustard
plasters when I should not
sweat or play with strangers.
I kept my hands to myself.
In spring there was never
swimming but there were long
summers in the Poconos, far
from the urban cloud of polio.

I learned to drive
slow but drove fast
as Father, straight as Mother.
The streets all ran
out into the white sand.
Between lesions
along the Fury's hood,

I would sight the dark
ocean like a marksman—

vowing never to love
the way we used to love.

II
A NEW SYMMETRY

WILD LIGHT

Wild rice is
watergrass
Indians gather at
lake borders
in northern Minnesota.

Similarly, wild
orange is the laurel
cherry, its flowers
milky white, the fruit
black and sleek.

With its rose
colored cluster of flowers
loose to breeze,
the wild hollyhock is
checkerbloom.
Yes,
and the rooting
stems that creep must
mean wild sweet william
is blue phlox.

You can see wild
carrot is Queen Anne's lace,
the broad umbels of white
flowers like a plum-stained
linen on the field,
and the white wild
pink is moss campion.

Wild tomato
is the bloodberry
as wild rocket is
hedge mustard as wild
rosemary is crystal tea

and as I
once
entered the wild light
and named it love.

MOTHER AND CHILD

Inside the mist tent our boy
is crying. Though muffled,
it makes her milk flow.
He coughs and sputters.

They have said she could,
so she lifts the edge
of the tent and gently leans
in beside him, moving fast,
knowing she is letting out
essential, saturated air.

On one side, both breasts
bared this time for efficiency,
her arm cushions him
as he finds her with a smack
and soft murmur.

She shifts him soon,
before he falls asleep,
and it is as though they both
are locked in a magician's
trunk heaved in water.
How quickly she mastered
the moves. Without glasses,
shrouded in mist, crying,
she cannot see anything.

When she emerges,
halters her breasts

and shakes her frayed,
dripping hair, neck
streaked with moisture,
I look at her and cannot speak,
cannot blink or move my eyes.

GIFTSONG

I gave my love a watch,
    loose green
tea (in a tin box
    I'd once seen
her handle when we stopped
    for whole bean
    coffee and spice),
        fine rice
paper, and made her Scotch
    woodcock
    for breakfast in bed.

I gave my love a game,
    rare sheet
music (songs which became
    obsolete
long ago but give the same
    old bittersweet
    pleasure now),
        highbrow
novels, and batiks that came
    with frames
    we must have painted red.

I gave my love a robe,
    hand-thrown
stoneware (made by an old
    woman we'd known
from Sedro Woolley who sold
    me the bone

39

colored set for a song),
two long
stemmed roses, and told
her bold
stories of the night ahead.

HAZARDS

Stiffly, without flutter,
her dresses, jeans
and creepers move
in the fall breeze.
She toddles beside me
pointing to jays on
the roof until the walk
ends, spilling her face
first in the grass.

I have seen cars
spinning toward her,
buses sucking her under
as she reaches up for me.
Derailed trains flip,
bounce twice, coming.
From left field, I have
seen fouls crack her soft
skull, seen dogs attack, bats
fly end over end to find
the blanket where she sits.

She is up, clutching
my finger, steadied.
A squirrel bursts from fence
to tree. She lets go
and moves toward it,
laughing, waving.

MY DAUGHTER CONSIDERS HER BODY

She examines her hand, fingers spread wide.
Seated, she bends over her crossed legs
to search for specks or scars and cannot hide
her awe when any mark is found. She begs
me to look, twisting before her mirror,
at some tiny bruise on her hucklebone.
Barely awake, she studies creases her
arm developed as she slept. She has grown
entranced with blemish, begun to know
her body's facility for being
flawed. She does not trust its will to grow
whole again, but may learn that too, freeing
herself to accept the body's deep thirst
for risk. Learning to touch her wounds comes first.

A WORKING MARRIAGE

No hardy phlox or spice pinks in neat rows.
Ragged lawn with untrimmed hedge, wasted space,
no garden. One more sultry spring. No time
for rest, day and night thick with choice. Nothing
on the wind but must, nothing in the way
of movement. The one truth is urgency.

Up at five, worksheets still spread. Urgency
wafting like smoke wakes the spouse. Two rows
of claret stains trickling down the stairway
mark their path to bed. Coffee brews. No space
for cups, no hunger or chitchat. Nothing
to be gained by touching; there may be time

later. They work in separate rooms, time
showers around toast and the urgency
of soft-boiled eggs. Outside, jays with nothing
to stop them seize the backyard, their harsh row
almost distracting. Squirrels sprint through space
a phone cable makes in elm leaves. The way

one's tail twitches before she runs away
makes her mate move through leaves like wind. No time
to lose, nothing on paper yet but space,
nothing quite as clear as the urgency
to look back from the window, start a row
of words down another sheet with nothing

on it. There are needs to project. Nothing
adds up. Footsteps of their child are the way

they know morning is relative. His row
of days leads mark by mark toward summertime,
weeks squandered, play the only urgency.
He eats toast and cheese in a cleared space

among flowcharts, ignoring the tense space
before the rush to scatter. Now nothing
can wait. Lights and locks. All is urgency.
Briefcase and thermos, hugs on the driveway,
all words becoming a matter of time.
They use sidestreets to bypass docile rows

of cars in their way, quick turns to make time.
Nothing can compete with the urgency
of desks without free space, stacks in long rows.

KALEIDOSCOPE

My child at two would not accept
the shut eye and peephole. I faced
her to light. I spoke of mirrors
and ground glass, covered her hand
to rotate the tube as I peered
describing patterns. But it did
no good. Because the toy shook noise,
she stashed it with her horn and drum.

*

That was your first house, a red and white bungalow, leaky, and we
lived there less than a year. This one was where you learned to walk,
tasted snow, hid in an empty carton of Scotch. Here is the house
where you blew fires to life with bellows. This one was the house
with the snake from the cornfield, the cord of wood left on the
porch when we moved. And this house was rambling and shaded by
twenty evergreens. It is the one we hated most to leave so far. We
have been here the longest.

*

The harbor busy at dusk.
Sourdough loaves, cracked crab,
steaming broth between us.
Herring gulls circled trawlers
back from the Straits,
notes from a hammered dulcimer
merging with their bugling.

She sprinted out the pier,
leaving my wife and me
our crust, shells and dregs.

45

*

There were steam plumes from volcanoes
There were rivers red with spawning salmon

There were no old houses
There were no seasons

There was rain so often
There was light so late

There was more time than ever
There was more stillness than peace

And I could not see the breach
And I could not name the dread

*

Your mother designed this patchwork
quilt the year you were born. She used
only four colors of fabric
and three shapes to make seventy
squares whose patterns do not repeat:
each unit distinct, same colors
never touching, the letters shaped
and filled with embroidery
stitches, forms and figures varied,
the whole making its own solid
symmetry. You could learn from this
the joy of touch, the warm comfort
of down, the sheer delight of home
made things. Maybe a time will come
again when I can look at it
simply myself, let its balance
stand for nothing except itself.

*

My wife's father
posed in the bole
of a beached tree
staring to sea.

My wife's mother
wrapped in a shawl
at Paradise,
pale scarf blowing
above her white
hair, the drought-blotched
peak above her.

My daughter with
a starfish cupped
in a clamshell,
the sky a wash
of gray, the waves
white behind her.

My wife beneath
the lintel leaning
with clasped hands
against the frame,
smiling as I
bring her into
focus and count.

Myself able
to record these
images then,
able to see

them now, although
in the mornings
the smell of my
own clothes inside
the closet brought
sudden crying.

*

A stack of flattened boxes in the attic. One shelf for bric-a-brac
salvaged after the movers' negligence and glued, braced, doweled,
taped. A roll-top desk from Carbondale, stoneware from Seattle,
lamps from Lancaster, chests from Olympia. A new round of
appliances. We must insulate. We must scrape and paint. We must
carpet, drape, shutter, vent, jack, grout, caulk, paper, prune, rewire,
repipe, reroof.   .

*

The paradigm of departure: suitcase
open on the bed, drawers slamming, doors.
Comforter balled on the floor, pillows
askew, a small box missing from the bedside
table. Wordlessness of the dire rift.

Or the slow walk through snow,
the hooded back seen hunched
against cold from my window.

Or the child held high
waving as the train leaves,
all three in tears.

Or cress-colored light and rain
through the Douglas fir. Alone
in the frameless bed, one set

of pillows propped in its center,
the other visible on the closet floor.

I might find a new
symmetry if I turn
the long tube of memory
and look again.

*

She ran to light.
The old toy we found
unpacking made sense
at once. She twisted
and turned, face
to the sun, silent
with her new vision.

Steersman with sextant,
she appeared able
to guide me to haven.
The juncture passed
but I held her still
as long as I could,
to hide from her,
to savor her certainty
that each new pattern
would be beautiful.

OLD STORIES

The second decade
of marriage is the living
room redone off-white, the rocker
in the attic. It is an oak
dresser stripped
and sanded, a roof
job, snow-in-summer
for ground cover.
The windows stay open
through November
and woolen wraps emerge sooner.

It is worknight
sesame oil rubs, kiwi
fruit sliced thin mixed with apricot
in plain yogurt, bikini shorts
for the first
time. Silk sheets and jazz
suites, ratatouille
instead of roast beef.

Forty approaches.
It is the time apart, not
the time together. It is loose
skin, the six-mile run after work.
No papers
and sweet rolls Sunday

mornings. It is the tin
anniversary,
new wrinkles in old
stories, the text
hand-set and stitched, not perfect bound.

SEPTEMBER FRUIT

This autumn my daughter discovered plums.
She found pineapples, figs, and blackberries,
learned to savor the pleasure that comes
from such summer fruit as sour cherries
in late September. I saw her eyes turn
inward, closing round a vision of lush
casaba. Soon she grew her thick auburn
hair longer. She began to love the hush

of held breath as her body welcomed new
tastes, risking flame tokays and tangerines.
I saw there was little for me to do
but stock apples and pears too. At fifteen,
she felt the world become hers to harvest,
welcoming each new flavor as though blessed.

THE STAGGER

The staggered start makes him
seem behind when the gun
goes off. He is slow to
rise from his crouch and hits
full stride well after all
the others. But I have
faith now in his power,
showing itself as he
moves at his own sure pace.

I love to see my son
running the turn, making
up the stagger before
the straightaway. He leans
in slack-faced, knees lifting,
claiming the inside lane
with his natural speed.

In his seventeenth year,
when I least expected
it, he has given me
a way to see him leave
childhood clear. There is no
tension in his body
as the finish line nears.
He sees it and maintains
good form, running as if
there were no tape to break.

THE BOW

In the attic, behind gray metal
filing cabinets crammed with defunct
warranties and canceled checks,
I found the recurved lemonwood
bow I bought the year I met
my wife. Its leather finger
and forearm guards still hung
on a nock. The bowstring looped
through dust and the quiver
folded in on itself beneath
the window that was losing
its winter light by the minute.

Some mornings the bow was
all I brought back,
slowly leaving my life
in her care, burying its
worst moments like the arrows
I would lose in the long grasses
behind her country home.
I loved to draw the bowstring
arrowless to the anchor point,
to hold still—forefinger brushing
my beard—and sight the mist
rising at daybreak before I left
for a house I lived in by myself.

The bow's belly is a shade
lighter than its back and shows
crosswise cracks. Its handle

is marked by the flight
of arrows aimed at paper
foxes tacked to hay bales.
After twenty years, I doubt
my aim. But it feels right
to take the bow in my hands
again, to flex it against
my foot, to ease the string
in place and carry it out
into the long fields
that border our life.

IN THE COAST RANGE

The clear-cut where my daughter sits
could be forest again, but not
in my lifetime. There is
no hint of water or new growth,
only bleached chips scattered
among stones. A folded shirt
cushions her from the rubble
into which her bare feet have dug.

She climbed this slope
somewhere in the Coast Range
with friends who know more
about her thoughts than I do.
She leans back on her own
hands for support, looking down,
I imagine, toward the sea.
A breeze stirs her hair
and nothing else.

Beyond her, I see the evergreen
looming on the next ridge.
I see them fade south
until they merge
with the morning sky.

SURPRISE VALLEY

It may be real,
                 a small town
in northern California
with a view of Mount Shasta.
It may be where people stop
for sparkling water with lime
on summer afternoons to
brace themselves for Nevada.

Over Breathless Creek, a cedar
footbridge there since pioneer
days.
            Daily rains soft as mist
make the woods lush, the berries
fat as pears. They are darker
than the nights this valley is
known for.
                 Ebonyberries.
Let's say ebonyberries.

Then suppose Surprise Valley
lies between the Range of Awe
and the Confusion Mountains.
Maybe Desolation Peak
hovers above haze-shrouded
foothills on hot days, faintest
at noon when there is a glow
on the rest of the valley.

This is where trees grow wider
than high, roads circle the source
of water in the town's heart.
It is a place without signs,
a haunt even for strangers.

Here is the summer breeding
range of the cinnamon teal
seen in the season his name
makes no sense until you catch
the males' bright peeps and forget
the fact of their drab eclipse
plumage.
           Only the sleepers
have no dreams here. The sleepless
see glaciers begin their next
move, have an inkling of what
the rest of us sleep to lose.

We have almost made ourselves
free. You know Surprise Valley
is where love, long since given
up for lost, is seen again.
Furtive at first,
              but in time
real enough for you and me.

YOU ASKED FOR IT

Show me film clips of William McKinley.
Show me Charles Atlas pulling six autos
down two miles of road. I would like to see
the vault at Fort Knox, chimps with hammertoes,
a man boning chickens while blindfolded.

Show me Ebeye Atoll, near Kwajalein,
worst slum in the Pacific. Show me red
squill being made into rat poison, pain
free surgery as performed in Shansi,
old friends playing poker underwater.

Then show me love as it was meant to be.
Show me an old man and his grown daughter
walking alone near a cranberry bog,
not the Robot Man and his Robot Dog.

SAPPHIRE FANDANGO

We mastered the azure
        fandango
early in our marriage,
        those high sky
days when we thought simple
        triple time
blazoned the purity
        of blue dance.
It was nothing for us
        to gain speed
like a summer storm—our
        castanets
clicking as if of their
        own free will
        as we moved
toward the moment of song.

Soon there was a gaudy
        interlude
of turquoise fandango,
        all opaque
and pulsing with guitar.
        We became
artless motion under
a wash of flickering
        seawater
light, lost till we chanced on
        the damson
fandango—its sudden
        stops said what

we had forgotten to—
    a dance blue
    enough but
reddened to plum as though
    rinsed by blood.

From there it was not far
    to the dark
duet we now perform
    with the best,
our sapphire fandango
where the passion lies in
    the absence
of motion. Between us,
    we hold such
stillness that music seems
    unlikely
to rouse us. But then comes
    rhythm once
more, and deep blue movement
from our frozen center
    where only
hope could remain alive.

III

THE VIRUS

BRAIN SCAN

Be still. When the chilling rush of liquid
fills your veins, breathe in. As it turns to heat
deep in your bloodstream, breathe out. The acrid
taste in your mouth is nothing. Meadowsweet
light flushing the stark white walls as you slip
inside the machine means nothing—a short
term shift in blood pressure timed to the drip
of dye. Since the least movement can distort

the image, forget that your cradled head
may reveal a hard secret soon, the kind
of growth you fear. Forget the narrow bed
you're strapped to and the woman, safe behind
leaded glass, who adjusts it by remote
control. What matters now is the subtle
shading of mass, some new darkness afloat
in the brindled brain-sea. You must be still.

DIAGNOSTIC IMAGING

Like thin mist settled on the red divan,
the old man leaves no sign as he drifts off
toward his name. He floats past a young woman
who waits for her mammogram, through the cough
of a boy stacking blocks, over plastic
armchairs where someone who resembles me
takes up the optimism of a thick
novel. Technicians in no rush to see

what goes on inside us sip coffee by
carts dense with film. They dominate this place
of higher math, of dark techniques, where dye
seeping into new mass turns inner space
opaque and numbers flash. Sound waves tracing
the shape of organs map the deepest change.

They picture what each of us is facing,
the plain future we cannot rearrange.

MUSIC APPRECIATION

—For Eric Hosticka

What am I doing reading
about tone color and quality of sound?
Largo and *grave* blur to *adagio*
and no one I know pronounces timbre
properly. I listen to the oboe
offering contrast to the amber
melody of the violin.
Alone too long this winter
with the mysteries of disease,
some virus my doctors say
is deep but cannot name,
I learn to listen for music. A trombone
slides from brilliant to mellow
while strings quiver. Here the crescendo
to full orchestra. I may never know
what virus this is, what brilliant cell
rewrites the entire score
my body has followed for life, throwing
its symphony into chaos. It's somber,
but I'm learning to appreciate
this new tone, the discordant sound
that accompanies vital change.
I was thinking *vivace,*
but find that recovery runs
at its own tempo, and settle back
simply to hear the way
my being achieves its harmonies.

SOLSTICE

The fat pink
grapefruit half you left
for me this last
morning of my first
full year of illness

with its sections knifed
free from the bitter
membrane and the peel
thick as hope

reminded me
in its sweetness
of time held still
within

a taste of summer
this winter

a seed of health
however small
somewhere in my weakening
center

that you touch.

SONATINA FOR SURF AND SANDPIPER

I was thinking of our spattering sprints
along tideline and the madcap scatter
of sandpipers. The cool salt air gave hints
those mornings of long decaying matter

when we turned back into the wind and light
was defining itself against the sea.
Of course we never considered what might
be within that wind, or that I would be

unable, just two years ahead, to walk
a quarter mile without rest. Love, I was
thinking today of sandpipers' sharp *plick*
in flight, a flock the same light gray as waves,
their cries soft in the sound of surf. I was
thinking of time, what it is, what it does.

A SOFTER PLACE

At ten miles, when the wooded trail entered
a clearing and the sun bathed my body
in winter light, my drifting mind centered
on how soothing it was simply to be
running—easy as the wind-driven air,
fluid as the stream under its thin crust
of ice. I pranced a heedless circle there,
leaping like a horse gorged with its robust
life, then plunged back among the old-growth red
cedar and yew toward the fire lane that led
me home.   Now I measure every move.
                              Eighteen
months have brought me to a point of stillness
far beyond hardwood trees and evergreen,
a softer place, a thicket of illness
where my mind is held fast by spots of pain.
One day soon I will waken and the air
will be thick with scent of huckleberry.
The great blue heron that once nested where
Balch Creek rushes down will fly over me
again, aroused by my being there so
early, knowing what I have come to know.

THE VIEW

When the fog lifts I can see
a skiff at the tip of Ross Island,
its lone rower fishing for winter
steelhead as close to land
as he dares. I wonder how long
he's been sitting there
while I pass another sleepless
dawn in my chair, by what means
he piloted through the thick dark,
and whether he's had any luck.

A speedboat rounds the island
as though freed by the fog
but does not move him.
When the tug that leads a half
mile raft of logs passes between
us, I leave my window to find
binoculars, hoping he will
not be swamped by the wake.

There is so much that I do not see
from my window, so much taking place
within this false spring of my third
year of illness. If other people's
lives become my fog, I may never
find a way through to a sky growing
this quickly blue. He is still
there, coming into focus, and now

I can see that the skiff is
a fallen tree, its thick roots
still holding onto the island,
and the fisherman nothing but one
massive, heaven-pointing limb.

THE VIRUS

How is it possible for something to be not alive and not
dead at the same time?
—ANN GIUDICI FETTNER
Viruses: Agents of Change

I know this is not personal.
Like a windowpane latticed
with crystals of snow, I am
simply a host the virus uses
to enact its sole pattern
of growth. I could be rock,
a broth of monkey kidneys
and Medium 199, a block
of moss. I could be you.

Yet I have no choice
but to take this personally.
Living three years in a state
of siege, a protracted cold
war, I am occupied by an unseen
enemy. My secret codes
have been broken. Cells
that once bore simple copies
of themselves now bear virus
instead. I have lost control,
order is shattered, pockets
of resistance crushed one
by one. Sometimes all-out
war threatens. I could come
apart like an atom bombarded.

Personally, I have become
other, though this is not
personal. I have seen myself
become a factory of disease
spewing internal acid rain,
then become the polluted
stream. Slowly the banks
of self erode, each lush
growth that feeds there
turning sere.

Nor must I see myself
as a lover deeply betrayed.
It is a matter of being as good
as the next available body,
perhaps worn down at the wrong
time, perhaps missing the right
envelope of protein, but nothing
more essential about the self.
The virus does not need me
to live any more than faith
needs a body of truth
to thrive. Without me
it would be there still,
never quite dead enough
to forget, never quite
alive enough to kill.

HOME REMEDIES

—Virus: a Latin word meaning
a poison that disturbs the soul.

I

When I was your age
my liver got so sick
I could feel it press
the bottom of my heart.

The virus that made it
swell was large enough
to see with the naked eye.
When they drew my blood
it was the color of urine.

Then each morning I squeezed
the juice of half a lime
into a tall glass of hot
water and drank it down.
No virus can stand up
to a lime. Two weeks
later I was cured.

That was the summer
of 1943 and I have
not been sick one
day since that time.
My daughter has been
on limes since she was

weaned. It was better
for her than any vaccine.

So my advice is try it.
What have you got to lose?

II

I'm willing to bet your home
is filled with electro-magnetic
fields, which would explain all
your symptoms: the fatigue, pain
in your muscles and joints, brain
problems. It is well known
that static electricity causes
a person's hair to straighten
and makes you stumble on a breeze.

I'm willing to bet you have
a microwave, computer, xerox
machine and big screen tv.
Your vision is getting worse
because you sit right in front
of the screen, not the other
way around. Come to think
of it, you probably use
a curling iron on your hair.

I'm willing to bet you live
right under electric wires,
maybe near a substation
or radio tower. You depend
on the very things that are
killing you, my friend.
It's worth thinking about.

III

Peel a garlic clove by clove.
    Swallow them whole
one by one until you have
    to stop and then
dice the rest into tablets
    you can wash down
with raw milk. Rub them into
    creases of skin,
grind them to powder and breathe
    them deeply in.
Wear long garlic amulets,
    take garlic baths,
burn garlic incense and drink
    dark garlic tea.
Morning and night you can try
    one dipped in oil
as a suppository.

IV

Quit sugar.
Quit vinegar.
Quit dairy.
Quit bread and flour products.
Quit corn.
Quit caffeine.
Quit alcohol.
Quit chocolate.

Vitamins rev the body's motor so
quit vitamins.

The worst thing is too much acid so
quit fruit.

Anything that eats outdoors is polluted so
quit meat,
quit fish and fowl.

V

Please read the enclosed brochure
Please look over the enclosed testimonials
Please study this pamphlet

IT CAN SAVE YOUR LIFE

Heal yourself with nature's energy
Heal yourself with magnets
Heal yourself with nicotine

IT CAN SAVE YOUR LIFE

You are the Lord's trumpet in His watchtower
You are not alone
You are allergic desensitized filled with empty of

IT CAN SAVE YOUR LIFE

It's not expensive when you consider the alternative
It's not difficult if you really want to get well
It's not as dangerous as doing nothing

IT CAN SAVE YOUR LIFE

VI

Visualize little men
in white coveralls
scrubbing the lesions
from your brain.

Imagine a team
of climbers rappelling
the sheer face of your spleen
and see their axes chip
away the gleam of disease.

A phalanx of soldiers
trained in wetwork
shows your weakened killer
cells how to kill again.

This is best done
in a darkened room
to the later music
of Dmitri Shostakovich.

VII

To get well you must learn to heal yourself.
Since every self harbors its own secret
cure, you must close yourself off from outside
influence and look deep within to find
what you need. My advice is to listen
to no one, not even your physician,
but rather go off to some deserted
corner of your own soul and lie beneath
its palms, letting the sun of your self show

you all there is to know about finding
the lost treasure of your own well-being.

VIII

Embrace your illness
like the day-old infant found
abandoned on a logging road
late one autumn morning
that was given its rescuer's name
when it was at last out of danger.

SAYING WHAT NEEDS TO BE SAID

Lesion: an all encompassing term for
any abnormality of structure or function
in any part of the body. The term may
refer to a wound, infection, tumor,
abscess, or chemical abnormality.
—*The American Medical Association Encyclopedia of Medicine*

Brain lesions have left my lexicon scrambled—
or maybe it is my brain that is scrambled
and lexicon scattered to flecks of brainwhite—
words looming here and there like stars in a white

sky of negative night. If the world's logic
seems skewed, at least my brain has a pure logic
now, a wild crosswired beauty. So I say
broadcast the cremation when I mean to say

microwave the cream of wheat or say my blood
tests show amnesia, not the more common blood
disorder anemia. I walk into walls
and say I walked into the roof. There are walls

around abstract thoughts I crash into as well.
The mere concept of health has become a well
too deep to reach for words. I feel confusion
like mine can make sense, though. Take the confusion

when I say Xerox the laundry and Xerox
the lawn. Every machine is now a Xerox

machine to me, which is just another way
of saying what needs to be said anyway.

Sick three years, I have learned to look at the bright
side. You can see the darkest trouble as bright.
For example, I don't say everything twice.
I'd hate to be one who said everything twice.

IV
SEARCH

BACKGROUND WORK

The part is yours; do research
thoroughly. Go to rest
homes and study being old.
Select a voice but don't
exaggerate. See how much
their hands really shake, heads
nod, voices crack. Watch
them walk; watch them sit:
it is important to pick
out where infirmity strikes in
movement: the knees? Hips?
Ankles? How do they chew?
Always be careful not to
overplay this. How do they swallow?
It is essential to the total effect.
If you can, study patterns
of wrinkles; prepare to be ruthless
with what your own skin offers.

Next, build a past. Check old
newspapers to get a feel
for context, create a family,
have children die; give one
a crippling disease. Test
infidelity, religious conversion.

Then eat a meal with yourself old,
being sure to ask questions (try
to answer with food in
your mouth or a forkful

poised in air): are you
happy? Do you fear death?
What would you say if you found
yourself talking to yourself over dinner?
Because only after you have done
all this are you ready to learn your lines.

SHORELINE LIFE

We lived seven years
on a strip of sand,
a barrier island shifting
toward land in the hub
of storm-borne overwash fans.

Montauk sat like a saddle
on the south fork's backbone,
cut off from the tides by bluffs.
Cobble beaches at Hither Hills
were signs of ravage made
clearer still by homes
toppled into Shinnecock Inlet.
On Fire Island, low dune lines
from Kismet to Lonelyville made
the risk of flooding greater.

Our place was marked by slow
losses to windswept bayside
rollover. The sound
of surf was always in our ears.
Squalls fierce from their wide
fetch could transport a ton
of sea front in one bad season,
scouring all landmarks.
Steep dunes and salt marsh
grass signalled how fragile
shoreline life could be.

I spent summer hours repeating
the mad dash from a dune's toe
into chest-high waves, losing
my breath the instant I needed
it most. Each new year, walking
the profile of a beach braced
flat for winter, I surveyed gray
breakers building bulk for spring.

This was where my father
moved us after his city
life ended. He found us,
at last, a home that could
fade into air and water.

THE RESORT

—Long Beach, NY, 1982

No old men
in pastels, no nurses' aides
      walking blue-haired widows,
no pinochle, nobody in hats.
      Now the boardwalk
is a patchwork of blond planks
      and salt rotted two-by-fours.
Former ski ball stalls sell
shish-ka-bob in pita halves
      and beneath the rusted
Ferris wheel three heaps of gears
      weather like driftwood.
      The luxury
hotels are cracked, wanton shells.

      This was home.
This is where Grandmother died;
      there, Grandfather. It is
      a city without
      a cemetery, a barrier island
of sand, salt spray and gull chuckle.
      This surf, tamed by jetties,
      is off-limits without a guest pass.
      That is what
brick and stucco do after
      decades of neglect.
      A jitney
      without passengers idles
at the crosstraffic light.

Back for a week
to see that mother heals,
I meet no friends on the streets.
It is spring but there are
no ball games, no babies
in strollers,
nothing is being restored.
Condos and pools with
no water, tarnished supports
whose diving boards vanished
perch above the azure concrete.
The beachfront
bungalows list and settle
while graying trucks
once the color of July
cruise the shore for debris.

One night
half a life ago
I stood chest deep beyond breakers
and faced leaving this place,
its dark bulk of ocean,
its hulk of dunes
beneath a black summer sky.
East a buoy
winked red at land's end,
west the shoreline curved
upon itself and disappeared.
I swam toward the stars.
The seaweed
that brushed my thighs
was equally adrift in the rising tide.

NEW ENGLAND NIGHTS

I have not seen New England
nights in years, but windswept
dark on the Oregon coast, a spit
in the Straits of Juan de Fuca,
and steam at dusk from the peak
of Mount Baker. Then the nights
in Illinois, prairie becoming
sky, ice layered on tree
limbs, air crackling with energy.

I have not heard New England
dawns since, a child in the White
Mountains, I could hear
through the lap of lake water
Mother asleep in the next
room of our cottage. The sharp
chip of a purple finch woke me
to morning that would frost
the lawn in softened greens.

I have tried northwest
nights that blur and cloak
the Douglas fir on Mount St. Helens
and dawns in Port Angeles
waking to quick blasts
from a ferry leaving for Victoria.
I have left, further west
at Lake Quinault in fog,
the knock of radiator steam
in June, light beginning
to penetrate the lowered shade.

I have come to the thick heat
of sleep in central Illinois,
waking to crickets or a street
light's hum, the harsh horizontal
of a midwest sunrise, sudden
shift of season. I have come
to nights like tonight, tucking
in children, busy with travel
plans, thinking of a stick,
line and hook, trout jerked
from foam in a New England
stream years ago. Moon,
and myself dozing in a canoe
hoping to hold the night
close, drifting from home.

PAGANINI AND THE POWERS OF DARKNESS

She swore an angels' chorus
swarmed her pallet bearing
sycamore slats for the belly
of her unborn son's violin.
When others claimed to hear
Satan's heartbeat in his sweet
tremolo, she remembered ebony
for Niccolo's fingerboard landing
like grace around her. It gleamed
with the Lord's truant light.

He said she was not to speak
of that, nor of his packer
father playing mandolin
to the rapt child curled
by the fire. She must lock
his early scores in a strongbox
under her bed. Let them believe
a demon composed the music
in blood. Let them weep
for the brilliance of his
fiendish cadenzas that flickered
like the tongue of flame.

An odor of sulphur rose
from the wings, sharp
as the whip of his bow.
Despite a hint of vapor
from below, no one stirred.
In a vault under the dark

stage he tuned his strings
to the devil's chosen pitch.
By shadow of candlelight, voice
hoarsened with cancer, he practiced
his sinister pizzicatos.

THE VELVET GENTLEMAN

In his beige velvet vest
hammer in hand for safety
Erik Satie walks home
from the cabaret in dawnlight
singing parodies of his friend
Hyspa's risque chansons
mingling plainsong and dancehall
tunes to the hammerhead
beat on his thigh.

The thief stalking him
slips behind a wall
of wonder. The shivering
hookers sigh and turn
back toward Montmartre.

This is his moment
of bare textures, of grace
and simple melodies,
when Satie knows music
must be a mosaic
of harmonies that freeze
the soul. Soon enough,
back in Arcueil, everything
he sees will be lavish
with crisp lavender air.
It will be all too clearly
a late fall morning and time
for him to lie in bed hearing
what the birds have to say.

BLANCHE MORTON

Being neighbors with Gracie
Allen taught her heart's
logic, the aptness of an empty
envelope to tell mother no news
is good news, the wisdom behind
shortening cords on lamps
to save electricity.

Blanche forgot words gone
haywire were grounds for laughter,
learning to listen instead.
When Gracie told her there is
so much good in the worst of us
and so many of the worst of us
get the best of us
that the rest of us
aren't worth talking about,
Blanche believed her.

We watched and forgot
Blanche had four Harry Mortons
in eight years, understanding
one vexed accountant is like another.
We learned tolerance
as she did, agreeing that if Gracie
made sense George would be
selling tires. We could see
Blanche lived by joining in.

But this was TV,
not life. We knew
it would be a different story
having zany Gracie next door
instead of Paul Baron who got polio,
or downstairs instead of Ann Pless
whose poodle barked from dusk till dawn,
or upstairs where the Welches fought
over having to live in such a neighborhood.

MELODIES

The way melody fills
the mind of a man
trying not to forget a face

is the way faces fill
the mind trying to remember
melodies. In the moment

before sleep, when there is
a measure of wind through
the wild cherry, he might

imagine it is her moving
through the leaves that makes
their rushing turn tuneful.

She favored dark alpaca
sweaters perfect for her
blonde hair and ruby lavaliere.

He remembers her face when
she sang at their wedding
dinner. Twilight, brothers

standing on each side one
note ahead of her. A sweet
spring storm from the north

shook the clerestory windows
above the stage. He knew
the tune but not the lyrics.

His bride's long hands were
loose at her sides and his eyes
were seeing what her closed eyes saw.

THE MILL

Albers Brothers Flapjack Flour
mill is closed, its brick walls
flecked with weed, bays boarded.
Bottles litter the loading dock.

Across the road, a railroad yard
unfurls tracks that curve
through at grade to dead-end
beneath the mill's chute two
stories above. Little but wind
occupies the space where flour
poured. Grain dust once deep
as snow has blown away for good.

I stop running, tired in the heat,
feeling full of my forty years
till a gull lifts from the rubble
and soars to the mill's roof,
scraps dangling from its bill.
Its call, a clear chuckle
in the air, tells me what lasts
when all there is to do
is wheel around and dive back in.
My breath settles.
I step across the tracks.

VOICES OF THE SEA

> The sea has many voices,
> Many gods and many voices.
> —T. S. ELIOT,
> *The Dry Salvages*

The barker filling the boardwalk arcade
with promises played first base when I played
third. His hands were soft as a god's when he
dug low throws from the dirt. I heard he stayed
home, turning down an offer from Boston
so he could help his aging father run
the family fish market.
                              He tells me
knocking down metal bottles will be fun.
He thinks I can win my choice off his shelf
for the little boy there, or for myself
from underneath the counter.
                              Then I see
that he sees me. As the speedster from twelfth
grade hovers in salt air between the child
and man before him, his laugh becomes wild
as a gull's cry above the rock jetty.
This was the solemn boy who never smiled?

He makes me remember autumn's hoarse voice
at high tide heard from my porch, spring's voice
of sudden squalls and sighs as winter seas
surged against the low dunes. But summer's voice
still eludes me.
                              I have come home to hear

it once more, bringing my son and an ear
trained to other sounds. I wanted to be
beyond memory, to float without fear
again in the Atlantic at midnight
thinking of nothing more than the lone light
at land's end.
     I thought it would be easy,
coming back with my son, at last the right
frame of mind—everything in place to hear
what the sea was saying and make clear
the lost sounds that had long been haunting me.

SEARCH

Back eight years ago near Spirit Lake,
back when Mount St. Helens had its cone—
and based just on what he failed to take
from camp—we found this guy, all alone
and dug in above Dog's Head, before
he even got cold enough to pray.

We'd combed his tent. He left behind more
gear than we owned between us. Wet day,
blowing hard, but all he took along
were ropes, his guide book, and boots. So we
guessed he'd tried a rock climb. Was a strong
guy—lugged tons up to camp—and savvy,
the kind who'd hear when wind is saying 'Climb
a sheltered face.' He'd avoid spots known
for being greasy when wet or prone
to avalanche. He'd keep track of time.

We walked right to him like he'd lit flares.

THE PURE TONGUE

This field of sand held summer
bungalows painted sea blue each June,
painted ivory and violet, radiant
before the wear of wind and storm surges.
Our streets were named for months.
We would walk the years until we were gone.

From the boardwalk to land's-end
dunes grew and shrank with the seasons.
But here where steam dredges pumped out
marsh and the silt was buried beneath
pavement, where dunes were held flat
under wood brought in by elephants
a century ago, the old hotels
exposed their brick or stucco faces
to the surf. I remember at dusk
big band music drifted on the spray
of August Saturdays and women
in fur hats strolled arm in arm.

Here the Ferris wheel mimicked
tumbling surf while the whip
cut its figure eights. An arcade
rang with light in breeze that waxed
the back of my ears with salt.
There I played in the superstructure
of a bowling alley that has turned
into this stretch of strand.

I have come back to my city, built
on fickle ground as though its footing
were bedrock, to imagine it returning
to the pure tongue of sand it was
before. Home again becomes a natural
barrier, alive and moving toward land,
able to replace itself with overwash
as the level of the sea slowly rises.

But I know what has ended is
only beginning again. Luxury
living is already for sale here
where all I can see is a fresh
pour of cement the same drab
color as the heart of a wave.

About the Author

Floyd Skloot was born in Brooklyn, New York, in 1947. He is the author of two novels, *Pilgrim's Harbor* and *Summer Blue*. His poetry, fiction and essays have been published in *Harper's*, *Poetry*, *Shenandoah*, the *American Scholar*, the *Northwest Review*, the *Gettysburg Review*, *Runner's World*, *Poetry Northwest*, the *New Criterion*, *Transatlantic Review*, *Prairie Schooner*, and *The Best American Essays of 1993*. He has received fellowships from the Oregon Arts Commission, the Oregon Institute of Literary Arts, and the Illinois Arts Council. *Music Appreciation* is his first full-length collection of poems.

From 1972 to 1988, he worked in the field of public policy. Since 1988, he has been disabled by Chronic Fatigue Syndrome. Mr. Skloot lives with his wife, Beverly Hallberg, in Amity, Oregon.